# Why Does My Dog Always Stare at Me?

**John Alan**

Illustrated by
**Joe Eckstein**

Naples, Florida

Text copyright © 2024 John Alan
Illustration copyright © 2024 Joe Eckstein

All rights reserved. No portion of this book may be reproduced mechanically, electronically, or by any other means, including photocopying, without written permission of the publisher. It is illegal to copy this book, post it to a website, or distribute it by any other means without permission from the publisher.

Published by Simon Publishing LLC
Naples, Florida
www.SimonPublishingLLC.com

Cover & Interior Design by Imagine!® Studios
www.ArtsImagine.com

ISBN: 979-8-9894345-0-3 (hardback)
ISBN: 979-8-9894345-1-0 (paperback)
iSBN: 979-8989 4345-5-8 (e-book)

Library of Congress Control Number: 2023920702

First printing: January 2024

This book is dedicated to my family,
Nancy, Jill, TJ, Steph, and, of course, Brody.

Brody dedicates his book to his animal family and friends both past and present, Bentley, Jazmine, Honeybee, Ruby, Petunia, Calee, and all of the Connecticut and Florida critters.

Special thanks to my publisher Joanne and my illustrator Joe.

Why does my dog always stare at me?

He stares at me while I am walking.

He stares at me while I am talking.

He stares at me as I step through the door.

He stares at me as I do my chores.

He stares at me when I am taking a nap.

He stares at me when he sits on my lap.

He stares at me if I watch TV.

He stares at me if I climb a tree.

He stares at me when I am sad.

He stares at me when I play with Dad.

He peeks at me while we play hide and seek.

He peeks at me every day of the week.

He looks at me when I read a book.

He looks at me when I help Mom cook.

He stares at me on a rainy day.

He stares at me when the clouds go away.

Why does my dog always stare at me?

Because he loves his family!

## About the Author

**John Alan Snopkowski** was born and raised in Connecticut, graduating with degrees in secondary education and guidance counseling. His love for animals inspired him to write a series of children's books about his family pet. A former educator and a father of two, he currently lives in Florida with his wife Nancy and their dog Brody.

## About Brody

**Brody** is an energetic labradoodle with a personality to match. He loves going for walks, swimming, playing frisbee and meeting new people. His all-time favorite hobby is watching everything that happens around him.

## About the Illustrator

**Joe Eckstein** is the illustrator of over twenty-five books for children, including *Herby Gets a Life*, which he also authored. Drawing and writing stories since he can remember, he grew up in central Ohio, holds a Bachelor's degree in Fine Art, and has worked as a staff illustrator for a leading children's educational publisher. Joe lives in Florida and is devoted to the wife of his youth, Kristen. Learn more about Joe and his work at his web site, **www.JoeEckstein.com**.

www.ingramcontent.com/pod-product-compliance
Lightning Source LLC
Chambersburg PA
CBHW061402010526
44119CB00010B/232